# Ancient Magick for Today's Witch Series

# CANDLE MAGICK

## MONIQUE JOINER SIEDLAK

OSHUN
PUBLICATIONS
oshunpublications.com

Paperback: 978-1-948834-05-6

EBook: 978-1-948834-14-8

Cover Design by MJS

Cover Image by MidJourney

**Published by Oshun Publications**

www.oshunpublications.com

# ANCIENT MAGICK FOR TODAY'S WITCH SERIES

The *Ancient Magick for Today's Witch Series* is a series for modern witches to explore ancient magick, covering Celtic, Gypsy, and Crystal magic, among others. It offers practical advice on spells, rituals, and enchantments for today's use, incorporating natural energies and spiritual connections. With insights into Shamanism, Wicca, and more, it helps readers enhance their magickal journey, offering paths to protection, prosperity, and spiritual growth by combining ancient wisdom with contemporary practice.

Wiccan Basics

Candle Magick

Wiccan Spells

Love Spells

Abundance Spells

Herb Magick

Moon Magick

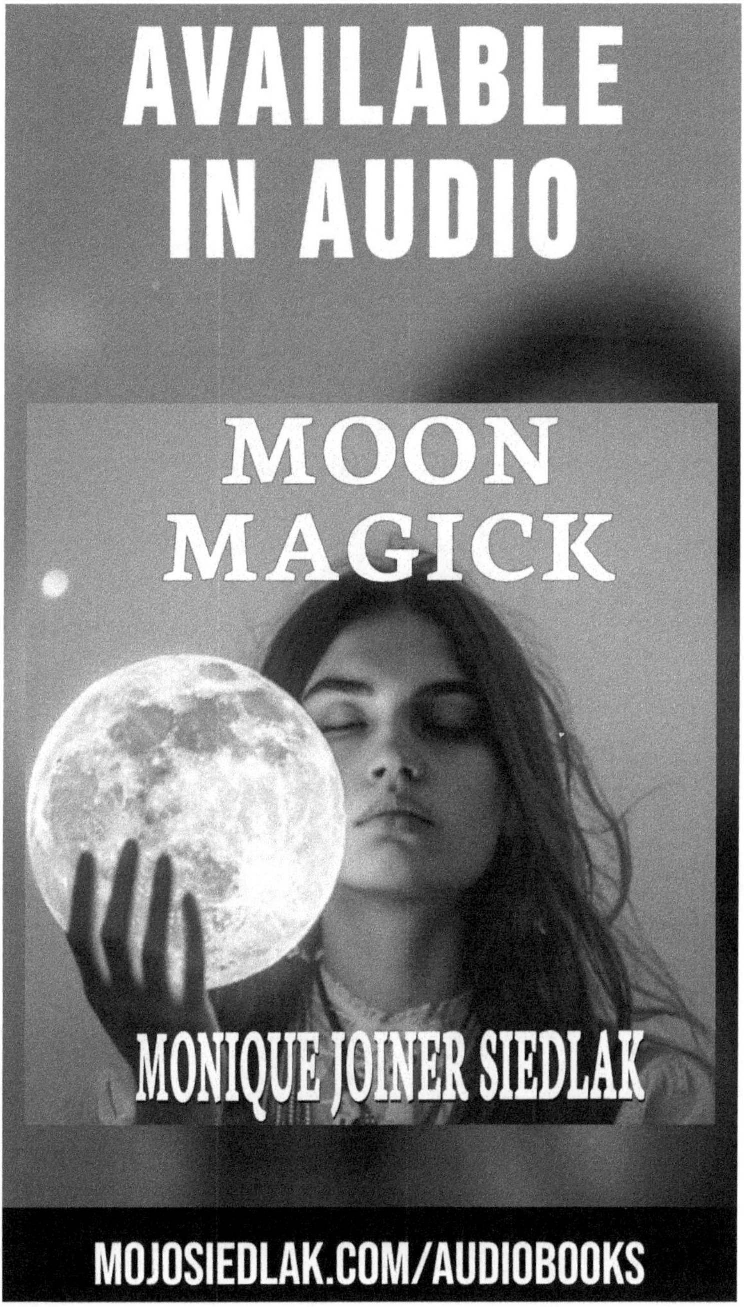

AVAILABLE
IN AUDIO
MOON
MAGICK
MONIQUE JOINER SIEDLAK
MOJOSIEDLAK.COM/AUDIOBOOKS

# CONTENTS

# INTRODUCTION

Candles have been used in magick for thousands of years, with candle magick evidence dating back to the Paleolithic era. Candles are a source of light, both literally and spiritually. They can be used in many ways to help you along your path in life, providing power, growth, and peace. This book will guide you through candle magick, giving advice on preparing magick rituals and what you will need. I will also provide a simple and easy step by step guide to candle making, accessible to everyone, no matter how craft-challenged you are!

The power of candles is witnessed in so many different religions and cultures. Including candles being lit on the eve of special days or used in ceremonies. Fire is, and always will be, a powerful tool for humankind. There has always been a magickal quality to it. It has the power to change itself and whatever lingers near it in the blink of an eye. It gives strength and energy, and it can take it away. Fire is beautiful, fantastic, and deserves respect.

Candle magick is undoubtedly crucial to Wiccan witchcraft and many other Pagan traditions. Candles are a staple for most rituals, and they appear in many spells. It is a spiritual tool and can be used to connect with the elements and our deeper selves. This book is to be utilized as a guide for those who are beginning their journey into candle magick. Still, it must be said that candle magick is accessible for all, not just those who follow Pagan beliefs. Whoever you are, regardless of what religion or array of spiritual beliefs you observe, there is energy within you to harness magick using candles.

For Wiccan witchcraft, candles are used to represent the God and Goddess on the altar. Candles also represent the elements. The solid wax is the earth, and when it melts, the wax represents water. The flame is the main element, and the air is witnessed to feed the flame. Harnessing these elements is essential to candle magick as they make up the earth and provide us what we need to make a change in our lives. Fire symbolizes many things but most of all, transformation.

Move into this adventure with an open mind and be ready to experience a new phenomenon and deeply implanted feelings. Candle magick will relieve you of modern society woes, bringing you back to a more grounded spiritual center. It will take earthly powers to harness them, a beautiful experience that is easily accessed through fire. Good luck! I am delighted to be a part of this adventure with you.

# 1

## HOW DOES CANDLE MAGICK WORK

To understand how candle magick works, it is helpful to discuss what magick is. For Wiccan witchcraft, magick is a tool used to connect with the gods and to nature. Magick is the act of focusing the mind to bring about change. It also opens up our minds to other planes of existence, allowing us to transcend the material world around us. Magick is available to everyone, as it is the energy of the universe that flows through us all. It is about focus and setting clear intentions. You do not have to be in a coven or strictly follow Wiccan beliefs to access magick. It is similar to praying, an act performed by religious practitioners and non-believers alike. There is a knowledge of some power more significant than you and I, and a wish for connection. However, it differs from praying in that way. The magick practitioner is actively involved with bringing about a change of energy, not just asking for it.

For a lot of Wiccans, there are many deities that we can connect with in magick. These deities are ancient spirits that connect and protect the earth and have done for centuries. The main two deities are the Goddess and the Horned God. The Goddess is associated with life and fertility, while the Horned God is associated with animals and the natural world. However, it must be said that there is a wide range of beliefs regarding deities amongst the Wiccan tradition. You do not have to believe in them to access magick. If you choose to connect with a deity in magick, you can pick the one you wish.

Magick can be practiced by anyone who follows a few principles that most witches have long agreed upon.

- Do not seek to harm others.
- Set aside all bad intentions.
- Attempt only the highest good.

If you follow these principles, magick will be available to you.

The transformational energy of fire is harnessed in candle magick. It is one of the oldest and most widely used forms of magick. In doing candle magick, we are inviting change into our lives. Fire is also a tool of illumination. When lighting a candle, we shed light on the world around us and, therefore, see our surroundings with much more clarity. In a hectic Western society, we are even more detached from the physical world we live in. It's easy to get wrapped up in social media, politics, work, and distractions the internet provides. But this prolonged behavior can have detrimental effects on our spirituality. When we are detached from the elements, we cannot use them to help us. We lose sight of our true selves, needs, and the innate link to nature in this detachment.

With candle magick, we can reconnect with the elements. This reconnection is vital for every living being, regardless of their beliefs. Witches, Christians, and Atheists are still people. Therefore, we all should be aware of the importance of the Earth and nature. How to tap into it for help when necessary.

Candle magick is an excellent way for beginners to start a reconnection journey, inner peace, and personal growth. It can be used for so many things and altered depending on your personal preferences. There is no limit to candle magick!

The reason candle magick works is by harnessing the energy of fire. In burning candles and opening up this energy, it can lead to an altered state of awareness, allowing the psyche and soul to open up to insight, positive emotions, and clarity. The candle's burning also sends energy out into the world in the form of messages or requests from us to the Earth. Candles access unseen energy from the Earth and harness it to act as a guide.

Candle magick is based on intentions and sending them out into the universe to be heard. When going into this form of magick, it is important to know what we want to get out of it. Using colors of candles, different carvings, herbs, and oils, we are creating a manifestation of our wants. In then lighting the candle, we are sending out these wishes into the universe, creating energy. As science tells us, energy is never created or destroyed. It evolves, taking on new forms, going on different paths. This energy that we have harnessed in the use of candles will come back to us in one way or another. Because we have guided it in a certain way, we will find the energy coming back to us in the form we wish. Candles are messengers to the earthly, spiritual world. It changes the universe and therefore changes our lives.

The simplest way to access candle magick is to light a candle while visualizing what you wish to achieve in the future. As the candle burns, meditate on this outcome. Your intention or goal needs to be clear and specific as things can go wrong if there is confusion on what you are attempting to manifest. It would help if you also were realistic, and it is better to break a bigger objective down into smaller steps. When it comes to candle magick, simplicity is key to help your mind and universe focus on the outcome.

Before you start your spell, meditate to quiet your mind and attempt to free it from worry and cluttered or mundane thoughts. Try and relax, bringing your mind to focus on the spell you are about to attempt. Bring this visualization to the forefront of your mind as you are lighting the candle. Some witches like to chant before they light the candle, repeating their intention aloud, summoning all the energy available to them forward. Some like to write out their purpose on paper and place it under or near the candle. It is up to you and how you prefer to harness the energy of the universe. There is no set rule when it comes to this.

When the candle is burning, take a seated position, watch the candle, or close your eyes. Keep your mind focused on the goal. Set the intentions, then send them out of your space and into the universe. Continue chanting if the feeling is still with you. If you want to stay silent, do so. If the spell is a one day spell, let the candle burn down safely, do not blow them out. The candle must be used only once. If it is a candle for a more extended spell and needs to be burnt for a specific length of time every day, use a snuffer to put the flame out as blowing it may scatter the intentions.

The strength of the candle magick, however, is ultimately up to you. What it unleashes depends on the power of your belief, imagination, and focus. Your energy must be strong enough to develop your magick, and with time and a little practice, you will start seeing changes around you. If you don't see an eventual change, keep working on your skills. Practice harnessing the energy coming from the Earth. This may seem difficult at first, as there can be confusion, mixed messages, or other issues, but practice amplifies change. Be positive, kind, and realistic. Visualize what you want, open your mind, and you will succeed.

Most candle magick is either personal or petitional. A personal spell is where you are sending the energy into the universe to accomplish your intention. This is where your intent is the main factor in which your magick will or will not work. It takes focus and a clear mind, but you will start seeing the change with more practice. A petition spell is where you ask a deity, ancestor, or specific god for help. Who you ask is up to you, but there is a lot of information out there on the different types of gods and deities. You can also ask an element for help in candle magick. These spells are good as your magickal energy is not drained; however, this might not always work.

In time you will be able to create more advanced spells as your magick gets stronger. To do this, bringing in more candles into the spell assists in its power. These different candles are representing the considerable energies, elements, people, and gods all impact your spells' strength. Advancement in spells also means you need to bring a different range of oils, herbs, and organic ingredients into your practice. As your knowledge becomes more advanced, your mind will sharpen. Your insight will broaden, allowing you to develop your own database of support.

**2**

---

# PREPARING FOR CANDLE MAGICK

Before you start your spell, you must gather the suitable materials. The preparations needed for candle magick are just as important as how you conduct the spell. The type of candle, color, and how it is dressed, all have significant implications for the universe's energy. Knowing the right candle to pick will get you on your way to powerful candle magick.

## Types of Candles

The material of the candle plays a significant role in candle magick. While candles can be made from various substances, those crafted from natural materials like soy, beeswax, or other earthly components are preferred. These materials are believed to facilitate a stronger connection with the universe, enhancing the flow of energy and making the spell more potent. Additionally, candles made from plant waxes are not only more environmentally sustainable but also resonate with the natural world, aligning with the principles of many magickal practices.

For those dedicated to the craft, Wiccan and witchcraft specialty shops offer candles designed explicitly for magickal use. These candles are often consecrated with specific intentions and can be more effective in certain rituals. However, practitioners can also find suitable candles in general stores, which, when cleansed and charged with intent, can serve the purpose well.

An important aspect of candle magick is the management of the flame. Traditionally, blowing out a candle used in a spell is avoided, as it is believed to disperse the energy and intention before it fully manifests. Therefore, when selecting a candle, consider the duration of the spell. For shorter workings, a tea light, which burns for approximately one to two hours, is ideal. For more extended rituals or spells that require a sustained release of energy, larger candles are recommended. These not only provide a more significant energy output but also allow the practitioner to gauge the strength of the spell according to the candle's size and burning time.

Including additional candles in the ritual can amplify the spell's focus and power. Surrounding the primary candle with others dedicated to supporting intentions or corresponding elemental forces can create a potent matrix of energy, enhancing the likelihood of the spell's success. This technique is often used to reinforce the spell's core intention, and it can be adapted according to the practitioner's needs and the specifics of the spell.

The choice of candle in magickal practices is more than a matter of preference; it's a crucial component of the ritual that aligns with the spell's intentions, the practitioner's desires, and the natural world. The materials, size, and additional elements all contribute to the spell's potential, making candle magick a deep, personal, and powerful tool for those who walk the path of the mystic.

## Altar Candles

Altar candles serve as a pivotal element in various spiritual and magickal practices, acting as beacons for summoning deities or harnessing specific powers. These candles are not merely decorative; they are potent tools for those wishing to dedicate their spells or rituals to a particular deity, thereby seeking divine protection or guidance. The luminance of an altar candle is akin to a signal, inviting the presence of higher powers or elemental forces to participate and support the practitioner's intentions.

When selecting altar candles, the practitioner's intent plays a crucial role. Each color corresponds to a different element or aspect of life, creating a vibrant tapestry of symbolism and energy. For example, a green candle is often used to connect with the Earth, symbolizing growth, healing, and prosperity. Red candles are linked to the element of fire, invoking passion, strength, and courage. Yellow candles represent air, associated with intellect, communication, and clarity. In contrast, blue candles, symbolizing water, are used for emotional healing, intuition, and purification.

The practice of burning these colored candles opens a gateway to the energies and blessings each element offers. For instance, water, represented by a blue candle, is crucial for emotional introspection and clarity. In moments of emotional turmoil or when seeking a more in-depth understanding of one's feelings, lighting a blue altar candle can facilitate emotional balance and guidance. Similarly, air, with its intellectual and communicative properties, is invoked through burning a yellow candle, making it an ideal practice before engaging in activities requiring sharp mental focus, such as exams or significant meetings.

Fire, symbolized by red candles, connects to our spirit, igniting motivation, transformation, and protection, whereas Earth, represented by green candles, grounds us, promoting abundance, stability, and physical well-being. These elemental associations underscore the vast potential of candle magick to provide support and empowerment across different facets of life.

Creating a sacred space or altar in your home for these candles enhances your practice, offering a sanctuary for spiritual work, meditation, and reflection. This space could be anywhere that resonates with personal significance and peace, such as a windowsill, a quiet nook, or a designated table. An altar becomes a personal retreat, a place where one can escape the hustle of daily life to reconnect with the deeper, spiritual aspects of existence. It's here that practitioners can engage in candle magick, meditate, and seek guidance, thereby finding balance and harmony within their lives.

Consider the importance of establishing your own sacred space. Reflect on what colors and elements you feel drawn to and how you might incorporate these into your spiritual practice. The use of altar candles is a rich and multifaceted discipline, offering pathways to personal growth, spiritual connection, and the harnessing of elemental powers to enrich and guide one's life.

## Astral Candles

Astral candles occupy a unique and profound place within the practice of candle magick, embodying the essence and vibrational energy of an individual. These candles are not just mere tools for spellcasting but are symbolic representations of the human spirit, likened to stars illuminating the cosmic expanse. Every person is a nexus of energy, radiating light and potential, and it is this concept that astral candles aim to encapsulate. They serve as a conduit for projecting one's desires, ambitions, and spiritual requests into the universe, leveraging the transformative power of fire to bridge the mundane with the mystical.

When embarking on spellwork concerning oneself or another, incorporating an astral candle alongside the primary spell candle magnifies the intent and personal connection to the magick being wrought. By allowing both candles to burn to completion, one symbolically releases their wishes into the vastness of the universe, trusting in the forces at play to manifest these desires.

The selection of an astral candle is a personalized process, with various factors influencing the choice. Pillar candles are a favored choice for their substantial presence and longevity, serving as a sturdy foundation for the energies being channeled. The color of the candle is of paramount importance, as it reflects the individual's identity and the nature of the spell. Many practitioners choose colors corresponding to the person's zodiac sign, tapping into the inherent qualities and energies associated with astrological influences. Alternatively, colors may be selected to resonate with the aura or emotional state of the person represented, ensuring a harmonious alignment of energies.

Customization of the astral candle through the carving of initials or zodiac signs further personalizes the candle, imbuing it with the essence of the individual it symbolizes. This act of inscription not only marks the candle as a distinct extension of the person but also serves to focus the practitioner's intent, reinforcing the connection between the candle's flame and the individual's spirit.

The practice of using astral candles underscores the deeply interconnected nature of the individual with the broader universe. By recognizing ourselves as luminous entities within an infinite cosmic dance, we acknowledge our power to influence and be influenced by the energies that saturate all existence. Astral candles remind us of our own inner light and the potential we hold to enact change, both within our lives and the wider world.

Including astral candles in spellwork is more than a ceremonial act; it's a profound affirmation of one's place in the universe and a declaration of intent to the cosmos. As these candles burn, they not only carry our desires into the ether but also reinforce our understanding of ourselves as integral components of the cosmic tapestry. Through the mindful preparation and use of astral candles, practitioners can deepen their connection to the universe, harnessing the elemental power of fire to illuminate paths forward, open doors to possibility, and enact meaningful transformation in their lives and the lives of those for whom they cast spells.

## Figure Candles

In the diverse and richly symbolic world of candle magick, figure candles stand out for their unique ability to embody specific intentions, energies, and deities through their forms. These candles, meticulously molded into various shapes, offer practitioners a direct visual and spiritual connection to the focus of their spell or ritual. Each figure, be it a representation of a deity, animal, or symbol, is chosen for its resonance with the practitioner's desired outcome, adding a layer of depth and specificity to the magickal work.

Burning a candle shaped like a woman, for instance, is a powerful practice within many traditions for invoking the Goddess's presence. This act is not merely symbolic but is believed to facilitate a direct communion with divine feminine energies, enhancing the practitioner's ability to channel these forces for healing, empowerment, and manifestation. The feminine form, with its connotations of creation, nurturing, and intuitive wisdom, serves as a potent focal point for spells related to fertility, emotional healing, and the strengthening of one's connection to the Goddess.

Likewise, candles molded in the likeness of a cat carry their own set of associations and powers. Cats, revered in many cultures for their mystical qualities, are seen as protectors against negative energies and entities. A cat-shaped candle, therefore, becomes a powerful talisman against evil forces, aiding in the breaking of hexes and the reversal of black magick. Its burning signifies the practitioner's intent to purify the space and shield themselves or others from harm.

The use of figure candles extends beyond these examples, encompassing a wide range of forms, each with its own purpose and symbolism. Dragons might be invoked for strength and protection. At the same time, a pair of intertwined figures could be used to foster love and harmony between partners. The selection of a specific figure candle is guided by the practitioner's needs and the nature of the ritual, allowing for a highly personalized approach to magick.

These candles can be found in specialized Wiccan and occult shops, where they are often consecrated for specific uses. However, the true power of a figure candle lies in the personal connection the practitioner establishes with it. Many choose to anoint their candles with oils, inscribe them with runes or symbols, or charge them through meditation, imbuing them with personal energy and intent before the ritual.

The act of burning a figure candle is visually and symbolically striking, creating a focal point for the practitioner's will and desire. As the candle melts, it is believed that the barriers between worlds are thin, allowing the spell's intent to manifest more readily in the practitioner's life. This process is not only magickal but deeply therapeutic, offering a tangible way to externalize and process desires, fears, and aspirations.

Figure candles represent a dynamic and interactive approach to spellcasting and ritual work. Their use allows practitioners to engage with the magickal realm in a direct and personal way, harnessing the power of symbolism and form to bring about desired changes in the physical and spiritual worlds. Whether seeking protection, healing, or communion with the divine, figure candles offer a path to deeper understanding and empowerment, illuminating the magickal potential inherent in all things.

**Knotted Candles**

Knotted candles represent a fascinating and specialized aspect of candle magick, embodying the concept of incremental spell-casting; unlike traditional candle magick, which often involves allowing a candle to burn continuously or until the spell's completion, knotted candles are designed explicitly for spells that unfold over some time. Their unique structure and usage underscore a systematic approach to magick, emphasizing patience, timing, and the gradual build-up of energy.

A knotted candle typically features seven knots or notches, each corresponding to a day of the week, making it ideal for spells intended to manifest over seven days. This design is particularly favored by Wiccans for week-long rituals but can be adapted to various traditions and practices. The process involves lighting the candle daily, allowing it to burn until one knot has been consumed by the flame, and then extinguishing it. This ritual is repeated each day at the same time, ensuring that the spell's energy is consistently nurtured and allowed to grow in strength and focus.

The incremental nature of knotted candle spells allows for a more controlled and focused release of energy. As the candle burns day by day, the practitioner has the opportunity to meditate on the spell's intent, reaffirm their will, and visualize the desired outcome with increasing clarity and power. This daily engagement with the spell promotes a deeper connection between the practitioner and their magick, enabling a more potent and precise manifestation of their will.

However, knotted candles should be used with caution, especially for those new to candle magick. Due to their powerful and cumulative nature, knotted candles can amplify not only the intended outcomes but also any unanticipated consequences of the spell. As such, they are generally recommended for more experienced practitioners who are familiar with managing and directing magickal energies.

For those ready to explore the use of knotted candles, it's essential to approach the practice with respect and understanding. Preparation involves not only the physical act of marking the candle but also the spiritual preparation of the practitioner. Cleansing the candle, consecrating it with oils or herbs related to the spell's purpose, and meditating on the desired outcome are all crucial steps in aligning the candle's energy with the practitioner's intent.

The application of knotted candles in spellwork highlights magick's dynamic and adaptive nature. By dividing the spell into daily segments, the practitioner can adjust their focus, refine their intentions, and even alter the course of the spell based on the insights and revelations that arise during the process. This adaptability makes knotted candle magick a powerful tool for transformation and manifestation.

Knotted candles offer a unique and powerful way to practice spellcasting, providing a structured framework for the gradual accumulation and release of magickal energy. Their use underscores the principles of patience, timing, and adaptability, encouraging practitioners to engage deeply with their magickal work. Whether seeking personal growth, healing, or the fulfillment of a particular desire, knotted candles can serve as potent allies in the journey toward manifestation.

## Candle Holders

Candle holders, often overlooked in their simplicity, play a crucial role in the practice of candle magick, serving not only as practical tools for safety and stability but also as powerful symbols and conduits for magickal energies. Their use transcends mere functionality, offering a means to deepen the ritualistic and symbolic aspects of spellcasting. As we delve into the significance of candle holders in magickal practices, it becomes clear that they are more than just accessories; they are integral to the focus, amplification, and manifestation of the practitioner's intent.

In the realm of candle magick, every element of the ritual holds significance, and candle holders are no exception. They do more than simply support the candle; they help to center the practitioner's focus and anchor the spell's energy. This focused intention is crucial for the efficacy of the spell, as it ensures that the energy is directed towards the desired outcome without dispersion. The act of placing a candle into its holder is symbolic of grounding the spell's intent in the physical realm, thus providing a foundation for the magick to manifest.

Moreover, the candle holder is often seen by practitioners as a representation of the Earth and the nurturing aspects of nature. This symbolic connection underscores the holder's role in grounding the spellwork and linking it to the energies of the Earth. Just as the Earth sustains life with its resources, the candle holder sustains the candle's flame, which is the focal point of the spell's energy. This symbolic relationship enhances the practitioner's connection to the natural world, enriching their magickal work with the profound energies that flow through all living things.

The choice of candle holder can also significantly impact the spell's effectiveness. Many practitioners select holders based on their material or color, aligning these attributes with their spell's intent. For instance, a candle holder made of natural materials, such as wood or stone, may be chosen for spells related to growth, stability, or grounding, reflecting the qualities of the materials themselves. Similarly, the color of the candle holder can be matched to the candle's color or the spell's purpose, utilizing the vibrational qualities of colors to amplify the energy. A red candle holder could be used to enhance a spell of passion or courage. In contrast, a green holder could be selected for abundance or healing work.

The consideration of color and material in the selection of candle holders is rooted in the understanding that everything in the universe is connected through vibrations. By aligning the vibrational energy of the candle holder with that of the candle and the spell's intent, the practitioner can create a harmonious and potent magickal environment. This resonance between the elements of the spell facilitates a more powerful and more precise manifestation of the desired outcome.

Incorporating candle holders into candle magick rituals is a testament to the practitioner's commitment to the craft, reflecting a deep understanding of the interconnectedness of all things and the importance of every element in the magickal process. As such, candle holders are not merely functional objects but sacred vessels that hold and direct the energies of the universe toward the fulfillment of the practitioner's will. Through careful selection and use of candle holders, one can enhance the strength, focus, and efficacy of their spellwork, further bridging the gap between the mundane and the magickal.

## 3

## COLORS AND MEANINGS

When picking a candle for magick, the candle's color is perhaps the most important element. Everything in the world has a color, and every color gives off different vibrations and energy to the universe. The frequencies of the color may be invisible to the naked eye, but they are felt. They affect everything we do. The pigment in everything around us releases energy, and we can use this in candle magick.

### White

White candles are usually associated with purifying and cleansing. Lighting a white candle is excellent if you want to empty your mind of worry and strain. They are great to use when going through a troubling time and wishing for inner peace. They are powerful and perfect for many different spells used in candle magick.

## Black

Black candles are a powerful tool, giving off strong and protective energy into the universe. By lighting black candles, you give them the power to protect you. They absorb negative energy well and provide strong psychic protection.

Black candles can be used with others during a spell. Because they dissolve negative energy, they can be lit alongside your main candle in the spell. This helps create a positive space for your spell to take place and remove bad energy that might be lingering around.

## Red

Red candles are mostly used in spells that encourage love, sex, and passion. The vibrations from the color red incite passion, the energy it gives off being lively and strong. This color allows you to connect to your desires, aligning your passion with the Earth.

Combining red candles with sweet things like sugar or honey can be a great passion relighting spell. If your relationship's passion is waning, a found spell like this one will do the trick. Light the candle with sugar or honey around it, and meditate on your relationship. The energy coming from the red candle will be accessible to you and your relationship.

## Gold

Gold candles are usually linked to wealth and power. Burning gold candles will summon good luck and fortune. It is connected to masculine energy and the Sun God and can be very powerful when used properly.

## Green

Green is the color of growth and is strongly linked to mother nature and her powers. It is a great candle to use for spells to help our personal growth. Sometimes we might feel at a loss and confused with specific goals and ambitions in our lives. We may feel stuck and unhappy. There is an element of renewal in the energy that comes from green, allowing us to see things from a new perspective.

Green is also helpful when we are practicing healing spells. Green candles invoke the balance of the mind, body, and spirit, which helps ground you to the Earth and connect your body to its surroundings.

## Blue

Blue is strongly linked with peace and tranquility and is a very spiritual color. Use blue candles in magick when you are searching for inner peace. When lighting a blue candle, sit with it and meditate on peace, where you are now in your journey, and where you wish to be. These thoughts and feelings will interact with the burning color and bring positive energy into your space.

## Yellow

Burning a yellow candle is excellent for the intellect and imagination. This is because it is the color of the element air and is potent in bringing about mental changes. It aids memory, healing, and creativity.

If you are an artist, writer, or musician, it is important always to have yellow candles available. They are perfect for dealing with a creativity block. With your dominant hand, rub a yellow candle with peppermint or frankincense. Place the candle in your candle holder and light it. Watch the flame burn and repeat this: give me creativity. After a while, close your eyes and visualize your ideal creative outlet or the one troubling you. Think about the projects you have finished and those you wish to achieve. Lose yourself in this imagination, and let your creativity flow. Do not blow out the candle, let it burn out, and keep your mind on your intention the entire time.

## Pink

Pink candles are brilliant in harnessing the power of self-love and self-acceptance. The energy they omit is tender and sensitive, bringing clarity to mind. Self-love is vital to most witches, and I strongly recommend using pink candles in your magick.

Sometimes the modern world drains us of our confidence. However, simple spells and techniques can bring it back, as well as promoting clarity and self-love. Lighting pink candles and decorating your altar with petals can be a good step towards accessing the powers of the Earth that provide us with the confidence we deserve. The good sensations and positive energy that the pink candles bring when lit helps greater achieve self-love.

## Brown

This color is strongly associated with the powers of the Earth. It represents femininity and strength, the source of life. It can be used to attract earth spirits and connect us to our primal and animalistic souls.

Brown candles are suitable to burn when you are trying to get to the meaning of something. Perhaps there is confusion over who you are, what you want to be, and what matters to you.

Burning this candle allows us to clearly understand what is at our core and our real wants and needs.

## Purple

Purple candles are great to light when you wish to meditate. The vibrations and energy that come from purple appear to help in unlocking psychic powers and expanded consciousness. This candle is great for introspection and spells that are about our personality and spirit.

# 4

## DRESSING A CANDLE FOR RITUAL

Dressing a candle for a ritual is of great importance when wanting the spell to be a success. When using candles for magick, we create a psychic link between ourselves and the candle. Preparing and dressing the candle appropriately is part of the ritual and will mean that our spells truly connect us to the energy we wish to use. By dressing the candle correctly, we are charging it with our intentions and willpower.

### Cleansing the Candle

Before you dress the candle, it is good to cleanse it. Dust and residue might have attached itself to your candle while being stored in your home, and cleansing it keeps the candle fresh for the spell. Wipe down your candle with a dry cloth, handling it carefully and with respect. If it is an altar candle that has been used before, take a knife to it and cut off any unwanted wax, making sure it is clean and ready for the forthcoming ritual. It is advisable to gently rub the candle with dried sage or lavender. Doing this means that the candle is cleared of any previous and unwanted energy that has been attached to it. It provides a clean start to your spell.

## Carving Symbols

Carving symbols and words into the candle is a popular way to reiterate and display your spell's intention. Using a knife, safely carve things into the candle wax that are important to you and the spell you are doing. Perhaps your intention is about work or a person. Writing a name or place onto the candle means that your intentions are displayed physically. This can help you direct the energy that is accessed in candle magick to the right place as it is clear what the spell is about.

When carving words and names onto the candle relevant to the spell, focus on your intention in a ritualistic way. Take your time with the carvings, channeling the energy that surrounds you. Focus on your intentions. Carving is a way to physically represent what is in your mind, allowing it to become something more tangible and malleable.

## Charging the Candle

Charging a candle for spiritual use can be helpful in magick, especially if you are a beginner. When a candle is charged correctly, it is infused with potent magical energy. It consequently means your spells are more likely to work. The energy used to charge a candle comes from you, be it positive or negative energy. It also takes energy from the elements, infusing it with your own.

The simplest way of charging a candle is to hold it tightly against your chest. This connects the candle with the center of yourself, and the energy that radiates from you goes straight into the candle. While you are clutching the candle to your chest, think about what this candle will help you achieve. Focus on the goals and intentions of your candle magick. Think positively and visualize what the magick will do for you. This positive energy will go through you and into the candle. Imagine your desires being fulfilled.

Take as much time as you need to charge the candle. You will know when you have charged it enough, you will be able to feel the energy emitting from it. Keep your focus on the positive energy that you have provided the candle with. When charging the candle, it is an idea to light incense to help with concentration.

## Anointing

Anointing your candles is an integral part of the process. Different essential oils can provide added support for your spell. It all depends on the intention of the spell. When you are anointing, you are personalizing the candle for your magick, securing the psychic link between you and the candle, making it even stronger. This means the spell will be more likely to succeed.

When you have selected the correct oil to anoint your cleansed candle, it is time to rub or anoint the candle with oil. Add oil on the pointer and index fingertips and hold the candle with the other hand. How you apply the oil is linked directly to your intention. If your intention is an invitation, calling a new form of energy into your life, start by rubbing the top of the candle. Then, move to the bottom, rubbing the oil in a clockwise motion. Then, finish off the anointing at the center of the candle, always clockwise. If the magick you are conjuring is banishment, you will anoint the candle differently. Apply the oil in a counterclockwise motion, again at the top, bottom, and middle.

Many shops sell oils suitable for candle magick, and there are countless online stores you can order from. Use oil that goes with the candle's color, increasing the energy and power of the spell.

For example, suppose you seek mental clarity or increased intellect, and purchase a yellow candle and use wisteria or mercury oil. In that case, both are known to stimulate mental faculties. Another would be in a spell for prosperity. You would use a golden candle and perhaps anoint it in bayberry essential oil with money granting energy.

If you cannot find an oil relevant to a specific ritual, olive oil or almond oil is acceptable to use. If you do not like using oils, you can anoint your candles with water. Most magic shops have a range of scented waters designed to anoint candles. Rosewater can be used for love or romance spells, whereas holy water can be used for protection. Apply the water in the same way you apply the oil.

If you wish, after anointing, would be the time to sprinkle herbs onto the candle. Certain spells require certain herbs, but mostly it is up to you and what you want. Herbs can be helpful when conducting a ritual. So when you are preparing for a spell, you should look into the specific benefits.

**5**

---

# WHERE TO PRACTICE

When you get started in candle magick, you need to pick a place for your altar. In paganism, your altar essentially means your workbench. Create your altar in any room of your home where you can be alone to practice. It is crucial that this is your sacred, quiet, and private space. This environment should remain relatively undisturbed and provide a heightened focus on the spell.

Your altar could be a mat in the corner of the room, or on your desk out of the way. Your altar must be clear of any objects that are not for the purpose of magick. It is advisable to have an altar cloth for surface protection and added decoration. It is good to have a few altar cloths that you can change depending on your performing ritual.

The altar's purpose is to provide you with a place to perform magick. It should include your herbs, oils, talismans, and an array of candles. Some people use this space to set their intention with decorated tiles or to draw daily tarot or goddess cards before meditation. It's also good to have one candle of every color at your altar and a few candle holders. Remember that your altar is unique to you and should be a reflection of your spirit and personality! Decorate your altar as you wish. When adding new things to your altar, remember to be aware of their meanings and energy. Cleanse with smoke when necessary.

Some like to include four items on their altar to represent the elements and directions of the Earth. At the north of the altar is a bowl of sand, dirt of a plant, this represents Earth. At the south end, there would be charcoal or a candle, representing fire. The east is air, so witches will often put a stick of incense on this side of the altar. Finally, at the west will be a small glass cup or bowl of water, representing water.

This is just to give you some ideas and get you started creating your altar. It is up to you to explore and develop your magick style. Remember to keep your space uncluttered and be aware that everything you put on your altar has a meaning and unique lifeforce.

## Care and Storage of Candles

The care and storage of candles are fundamental aspects of maintaining the integrity and efficacy of your magickal practice. Candles are not merely tools but sacred objects that carry and channel energies for spells and rituals. Proper storage and handling ensure that these energies remain pure and potent, ready to amplify your intentions whenever you call upon them. Establishing an altar for both the active use and the long-term storage of your candles not only organizes your space but also sets apart your magickal tools from the mundane, reinforcing their particular role in your practice.

### Altar as a Sanctuary for Candles

The altar, a dedicated sanctuary for your magickal candles, plays a pivotal role in maintaining their potency. It's not just a physical space but a representation of your commitment to your craft. The altar aids in focusing your intent during rituals and ensures you're always prepared with a variety of candles. The energy surrounding your altar and candles is crucial, making it essential to maintain this sacred space as a positive and powerful area, free from negative influences that could affect the potency of your magick.

## Tailored Storage Techniques

Wrapping candles in tissue paper is a practice that holds both practical and symbolic significance. It keeps the candles clean and also reinforces their magickal purpose. Matching the color of the tissue paper with the candle it wraps is a mindful way of further charging it with your intent, even when not in use. This careful handling signals respect and care for your tools, principles central to any spiritual practice.

Placing wrapped candles in a wooden box offers an additional layer of protection and energy insulation. Wood, being a natural material, resonates with the earth's energy, providing a harmonious environment for your candles. This method of storage not only keeps your candles in a pristine condition but also ensures they are imbued with natural, grounding energies, enhancing their magickal properties.

## Practical Considerations

The physical care of your candles is as essential as their spiritual management. Candles should be stored at room temperature in a place where they won't be exposed to extreme temperatures or direct sunlight, which could cause them to warp or melt. Ensuring they are kept in a clean, dry place also guards against the accumulation of dust or debris, which could affect how they burn and, by extension, the execution of your rituals.

## Safety and Suitability

Using suitable containers for burning candles, especially within a glass holder, is of utmost importance. Standard glassware may not withstand the heat generated by a burning candle and could pose a safety risk. Glass candle holders, on the other hand, are specifically made to tolerate the thermal stresses of candle burning, ensuring your practice is not only practical but safe.

The careful storage and maintenance of your candles are foundational to a respectful and powerful magickal practice. By investing time in the proper care of your tools, you honor the energies they represent and ensure your work remains potent and protected. Whether through thoughtful wrapping and storage or the use of an altar as a sacred space, the way you care for your candles reflects the depth of your commitment to your path and the success of your magickal endeavors.

## Wax Dripping

Wax dripping is a common issue for anyone who frequently uses candles, especially in rituals, spells, or even just for atmospheric lighting. While candles add an undeniable charisma and ambiance to any setting, the residue they leave behind can be a nuisance. Fortunately, there are practical and effective methods for dealing with wax drippings, ensuring your candle holders remain clean and ready for their subsequent use.

### Hot Water Method

One of the simplest and most effective ways to remove wax drippings from candle holders is by using hot water. The heat melts the wax, making it easier to wipe away or rinse out. This method works well for both metal and glass holders. Still, caution is advised to avoid burns or thermal shock, especially with glass materials. Carefully pouring hot water directly over the wax can loosen its grip, allowing it to be removed with minimal effort. It's essential to protect your hands with gloves and to pour slowly to control the direction and flow of the hot water, preventing splashes and spills.

## Freezer Technique

Another popular technique for removing wax is to place the candle holder in the freezer for about an hour. The cold temperature causes the wax to contract, often popping free from the holder's surface entirely or at least becoming brittle enough to be easily chipped away. This method is particularly effective for thick wax accumulations. It is a safer option for delicate holders since it avoids the risk of thermal shock or damage. However, it's essential to remove any residual moisture to prevent water stains, especially on metal holders that might be prone to rust.

## Preventative Measures for Votive Holders

When it comes to votive candles, which are notorious for leaving behind a pool of wax, a preventative approach can save time and effort. By adding a few drops of water to the glass before placing the candle, you create a barrier that prevents the wax from adhering firmly to the glass. This ingenious trick significantly eases the cleanup process, allowing the wax to be removed almost in one piece after the candle has burned down. However, moderation is vital, as too much water can seep into the wick and hinder the candle's ability to burn. It's also crucial to use this method only when you intend to light the candle immediately, preventing the wick from absorbing water over time.

## Candle Wick Considerations

The integrity of the candle wick is vital for proper candle burning. Introducing water into the equation requires careful consideration, as a wet wick can lead to burning issues, such as uneven burning, reduced flame size, or complete failure to light. Ensuring that the wick stays dry and is adequately maintained—trimmed to about 1/4 inch before each burning—can significantly enhance the candle's performance and lifespan, providing a cleaner burn with less drippage.

Managing wax drippings is an essential aspect of candle care, especially for those who utilize candles in their daily lives or spiritual practices. Whether employing the hot water method, using the freezer, or taking preventative measures with votive candles, each technique offers a way to maintain the beauty and functionality of your candle holders. With these methods, you can enjoy the serene ambiance and magickal atmosphere that candles provide without the hassle of stubborn wax residues.

# 6

# HOW TO CREATE YOUR OWN CANDLES

Making candles is a fun and creative way to connect to your practice on a deeper level. You can create candles specifically for any ritual. Making your own candles bonds you and creates direct energy flow to the ritual, increasing the magick's potency. Even more potent than if you bought the candle from a shop. Making candles is surprisingly easy!

In this chapter, I will guide you through the magick candle making process by using your personality and intent to create the perfect candle. Knowing you have made it yourself, infusing it with your energy, makes the candle's power stronger, meaning that the spell is much more likely to work. Once you have practiced a few times, candle making will become a natural part of the ritual process.

Learning how to make your own candles also means that you can create exactly what you need. Sometimes when looking for candles for a spell, I cannot find the right ones or something just feels off. Some spells need candles with specific qualities or an unusual mix of colors, herbs, or oils. This is why I began to make my own candles. It provides you with the means to have the perfect candle for any ritual or spell.

## Preparation for Candle Making

To make your own candles, you must first make sure you have a clean and safe workbench for the creation. I normally make my candles on my kitchen counter. A counter, desk top, or floor space can all be great workplaces for candle making, as long as they are sanitized and clean of energy!

Firstly, make sure that the area you are making the candles in is free of debris, dust, and clutter. Wipe down the surface with a clean cloth before putting any items down.

Now, you must cleanse the energy of the space, cleaning it from negative or unwanted vibrations. Set your intention. Say out loud:

**"This is my space for candle making."**

I frequently cleanse my spaces by smudging with sage. Sage can be picked up in most candle shops or ordered online. It is an essential item for anyone interested in magick or witchcraft! Light the sage, let it burn for a while, then blow it out. When the flame is out, and the sage embers are burning, gently fan it around your workspace. You might also want to place crystals around your workspace or light incense. This depends on your feelings and emotions and what you might need to concentrate on and immerse yourself in the candle making.

## Materials

Before you start your candle making, you must have all the necessary crafting materials. Some you might already have in your home, others you might need to go to a craft or magick shop or order online. Read through and make a list of what you need before venturing off!

Firstly, and most importantly, you will need wax. Some people use wax from old candles, but I don't like to do this as the old candles' energy could potentially impact new magick. I would advise using beeswax or soy wax and make sure they are naturally sourced. You can use dyed wax or add your own dye, depending on the ritual you are making the candle for. Making your own candle means you have the creative liberty to create the perfect shade of any color. Mixing different dyes and waxes in whatever way you wish. You may also want to buy specific herbs or essential oils to create a unique candle for spells.

You must also purchase wicks, and these can be found in most craft stores or online. Different types of wicks can be used. My personal favorite is braided cotton. If you are making thick candles, remember to use a thicker wick. It is also helpful to also purchase wick holders, keeping the wick steady in the container or mold when you are making the candle.

It is necessary to have a double boiler in candle making as the wax needs to be melted in a pot submerged in hot water. You cannot melt the wax on a stove or in a microwave, which can be dangerous. Plus, the double boil method means the wax itself does not damage or burn.

You will need a container for your candles, whatever shape you wish them to be. You can get individual molds from craft stores, or recycling old containers can be fun! Anything that can withstand heat can be used as a candle mold or container, so this is really up to you and your creativity in what you decide to do.

A thermometer, oven gloves, and a wooden spoon are all necessary for candle making. Scales also can be used if you wish to follow a specific recipe, but I like to go with the flow, and it comes out just fine.

## Technique

Now you have all the materials and the right workspace; it is time to start making candles. Give yourself an afternoon of candle making, so you can relax and enjoy this time; you never want to rush the process. Perhaps light some incense or put on some music. Creating the right atmosphere for candle making is essential for the candle to be fully infused with positive energy. Cover your clothes with an apron, or even better, just wear old clothes you don't mind getting a little dirty. Candle wax can be a pain to get out of fabric, and it can splatter on you, so don't wear anything that you are not willing to ruin. It is all part of the fun! Also, always remember to be safe. Never leave hot wax alone and never heat wax over 275°F. Do not let wax come into contact with flames, and always be aware of the wax's temperature.

## Melting the Wax

Cut or shred your wax down to smaller chunks. This makes it easier for melting. When it is suitable for melting, put it in the smaller sized pot. The smaller pot can be metal, or glass, depending on what you have to hand, as long as it is heat resistant and able to fit in the bigger pot.

Next, pour water into the larger pot, filling it about halfway, and placing it on the heat source, such as your stove. Then put the smaller pot with the wax in floating in the water of the bigger pot. Turn the heat on medium-high, so the water comes to a boil. The boiling water will then start to melt the wax slowly. When the water has come to a boil, you can then turn it down to a simmer. Keep a thermometer in the wax as it is boiling, and keep an eye on the temperature as you don't want it getting too hot!

For beeswax, let it melt to around 145°F. If you're using soy, it needs to be melted to 180°F. When it is at this boiling point, you can add any dyes and fragrances. Stir in what you wish, personalizing the candle to your spell. Remember to research what you are adding. You do not want to create any foreboding energy. Remember, all colors give off vibrations, and all oils and herbs have distinct qualities.

While you are stirring ingredients into the wax, this is the time to further connect to the energy around you, set your intention for this candle, and its use in future spells. Some take this opportunity to chant or sing their mantras or visualize them in their heads. It is entirely up to you how you strengthen your connection to the ritual candles you are creating.

Always stir in the ingredients right before pouring into the molds, so their potency is not diminished as they solidify.

**Molding the Wax**

Make sure that the mold you are using is at room temperature or warmer. If it is cold, the wax will melt unevenly. Before you put the wax into the mold, you must set the wick in. Place it at the center of the mold, with about two inches sticking out the top. Use a wick holder to secure the wick down onto the bottom of the container. Pull the wick taut. Some people wrap the wick around sticks or skewers at the top to hold them in place. Others prefer to keep them at the top with one hand, pulling tightly, while carefully pouring the wax into the mold.

When the wick is in place, now is the time to pour your wax into the mold. Slowly pour the wax into the mold, taking your time, so there are no spillages. When you have filled the mold up, secure the wick in place by wrapping it around a stick. Rest the stick on the sides of the container. You can also use a wick bar that can be purchased in any craft store along with other candle making ingredients.

## Cooling

When it comes to making candles, you must leave them to cool as long as you can, at least overnight. The larger the candles, the longer the cooling time, and sometimes a candle may seem hardened and ready to use but is still really soft inside. The longer you can wait until using the candle, the better. Bear this in mind when planning your spells and rituals. Make sure you give yourself enough time for the candle to cool thoroughly.

It's a good idea to leave them to cool in the place you have made them. Since you have already cleansed the area before making the candle and have focused your intention here, the area is full of the correct energy. With that, the candle can rest undisturbed.

Clean up the area of any remaining scrap materials, and wipe everything down with a cloth or paper towel. If you wish to store your candles, make sure you do it safely and with respect. If the candles are not going to be used for a while, the way you store them will affect their charge. When you are making your own candle, the act of making the candle itself is part of the magick process.

By creating, you are charging the candle with energy. Therefore, when you store your candles, be sure that they are stored safely and out of the way of any negative and unwanted energy that might alter their charge. Place them in a special box near your altar and look after them well until they are used.

# 7

# HOLDING THE RITUAL

Now you have got the candles, either by making them yourself or purchasing them from the store. You have selected the right color, right oils, and the candle is dressed, anointed, and charged. Now it is time to hold the ritual.

In this chapter, I will discuss the timing of the rituals and things you must be aware of when deciding when to proceed. The planets and the Moon all affect the energy in the universe. You must be mindful of these things for the spell to work. I will also discuss the meaning of different flames produced during the ritual. The energy the candle is putting out into the world will also reveal specific messages to you. It is essential to be sensitive to the sounds, shapes, and colors the flame presents.

## Timing

Astrological influences can affect candle magick. The more in tune you are to the universe around you, the more likely your candle magick will succeed. Magick is a part of the universe. It is energy and spirit. Therefore, the universe affects magick.

Working in harmony with nature, planets, and the Moon means that they will be on your side, sending the right energy your way. It is all about respect, awe, and love. We should aim to be at one with the universe, and candle magick is a way to do this.

## The Moon

The most extraordinary celestial being, the most beautiful and awesome natural satellite of this planet, the Moon has so much power over us, more than you can imagine. Her rhythm and cycles guide the seas and animals. She controls the tides, and she has been looked upon with wonder for millennia, giving humanity routine and protection. My favorite thing is looking up to the Moon and seeing the different colors on her surface. All the different shades of gray. It makes me feel so small but so significant at the same time. When there is a Full Moon, you cannot help but stare if you catch it. How many people do you know text their friends, "go look at the moon" when she is hanging so delicately and unblemished in the sky, glowing with reflection from the Sun? I know I do. She is one thing that all of humanity shares.

Being in tune with the Moon can help your practice. Throughout her cycle, she provides different forms of energy that can be harnessed. When there is a new moon, spells and rituals regarding fresh starts and personal growth can become more potent at this time. The Moon is not visible at this part of the cycle, but she will help you in your magick. Take the time for yourself during the New Moon. Think about the magick you wish to perform to assist you in your personal growth or any goals you may have.

The next phase of the Moon is waxing. This part of the cycle is where the Moon is getting bigger every night, from a crescent

Moon's silvery thread to a bigger and more fuller one. This phase is a great one to perform magick that aims to bring something into your life or increase something you already have. It is useful to conduct spells about finance, love, or careers at this part of the Moon's cycle.

The Full Moon is the brightest one in the cycle, incredible and brilliant to witness on a clear night. Here, she shines down on us, illuminating everything. This is where her power is most potent, so most spells are more powerful during this phase. Protection spells are especially potent during this time, as the Moon's energy can be connected with. The Full Moon lasts three days.

Waning moons come after the Full Moon, and this is when the Moon gets smaller each night. This Moon is perfect for spells and rituals that are focused on getting rid of something. Perhaps you need to banish something in your life or a part of your personality that you don't like and wish to rid yourself of. Now is the time to perform spells that tackle these things.

Other shades of the Moon include the blood moon, which happens to a full moon during a lunar eclipse, or a super moon where the Moon is full. The earth is close in proximity, so it appears much larger in the sky. Certain spells are designed to be practiced during a blood moon, and a super moon means that the Moon's energy is stronger. It is helpful to be aware of these celestial events, perhaps getting a diary or phone app that helps you track the Moon. More knowledge about the Moon means that you can forge a deep connection with her, helping your magick and witchcraft.

## Days of the Week

Which day you conduct your ritual on can have an impact on its strength. Different days are associated with different things. Therefore, it is crucial to be aware of these when deciding when you will perform your ritual.

Monday is ruled by the Moon and, therefore, a good day to conduct rituals or spells linked to emotions or femininity. Spells regarding domestic or family life can be more powerful when performed on a Monday.

Tuesday has strong, masculine energy. It is a day ruled by the color red and the planet Mars. This is a good day for spells that are based around courage, leadership, and action. If you need spell work to reverse hexes of psychic attack, do this on a Tuesday as there is a powerful and aggressive energy in the air.

Wednesday's color is yellow, and Mercury rules it. Spells regarding creativity and communication should be performed on this day. It is a perfect day to perform magick to aid the creative juices, helping you make art or music. Mercury also helps with spells regarding luck and trade.

Thursday is ruled by Jupiter and a day with a strong energy regarding expansion or growth. Spells or rituals regarding academic success or career goals will be stronger when performed on a Thursday.

Friday is the best day when wishing to hold rituals regarding love or friendship as Venus rules it. There is substantial energy on a Friday for helping romance and pleasure. It is also a good day to harvest plants or herbs that you might be wishing to use in future magick.

Saturday's colors are dark brown and black, and it has earthly vibrations. Saturn rules it. Magick being done on a Saturday can help your direct world and nature around you. It is also a good day for banishing spells.

Sunday is ruled by the Sun and the colors gold and yellow. It is a day for big, bold spells that invoke significant changes in your life. The power of the Sun is on your side but use it wisely. It is a strong force, willing to help those that will respect it. It is a day for renewals, affirmations, and beginnings.

## Planetary Hours

Similarly to the days of the week, hours of the day are linked to different planets. It is an ancient system, one used for centuries, but still can be used today to help us in our magick. The classic planets are Saturn, Jupiter, Mars, the Sun, Venus, Mercury, and the Moon. As the days progress, each one takes certain hours for rulership. For some magick practitioners, using the planetary hours to help rituals can be too much, especially as a beginner. It is not necessary but will help with strength.

For example, suppose you were conducting a ritual that is intent on passion. In that case, you might choose to do it on a Friday to harness the power and energy of Venus. To further make use of Venus's influence, conducting the ritual on a Friday during Venus' hours would strengthen the spell, making it even more powerful. Furthermore, this allows a spell to be influenced by other planets as well. If you are working on a banishing spell for someone with strength and power over your life, performing the spell on Saturday in the hours of Mars harnesses both the forces of Saturn and Mars. This is a potent mix for banishing spells, especially against a tormentor or aggressor in your life.

Planetary hours differ depending on where you live, but you can find charts online that are simple to use. Each day consists of 24 planetary hours and begins at dawn with the day's planet. The hours then proceed according to the next planet on the Chaldean order: Saturn, Jupiter, Mars, the Sun, Venus, Mercury, and the Moon. It must be noted that the hour lengths depend on sunrise and sunset, which you can work out yourself or find online.

**The planets and their link to magick are as follows:**

- In the hours of the Moon, magick regarding women or mothers becomes stronger. It also helps spells that are about communication, journeys, or messages.
- In the hours of Mercury, intellect and creativity are helped. These are hours that assist with spells regarding puzzles, school, business, and skill.
- In the hours of Venus, spells, and magick about love, romance, and friendship are strengthened. These hours are those of connection, communication, and harmony.
- In the hours of the Sun, most magick is aided with strength and power. Wealth, hope, fortune, energy, and reputation are all helped in these hours.
- In the hours of Mars, magick aimed to ward off aggressive or hostile enemies is strengthened. Banishment spells are more potent.
- In the hours of Jupiter, friendship and health spells are strengthened. Spells that consider influential people and connections.
- In the hours of Saturn, and magick linked to agriculture or the natural world becomes stronger. These are also times when magick aiming to decrease or eliminate negative things in our lives is supported.

# 8

# DIFFERENT FLAME MEANINGS

As you begin your ritual, light your candle. I use wooden matches for mine, but I don't think the way you light the candle affects the spell. It is, like everything else in magick, up to you. This is your energy, your power, and you can personalize it how you wish.

When the ritual is taking place, try closing your eyes to chant or visualize your intent. I do this occasionally, but it is good practice to keep your eyes on the flame. Not just because of safety reasons, although they are essential because the flames will tell you things.

As you begin your journey into candle magick, you will notice that flames have a language of their own. As you learn more, you will become in tune with messages and meanings behind the flames. Pay attention to how the flame bounces and how the smoke drifts as these all have a unique meaning. It is good to practice communication with the element of Fire.

When your candle is burning, watch it, freeing your mind of distractions. You will find yourself beginning to develop a psychic link to the flame, delving deep into the understanding of it. Only you will understand what the flame means and what it is trying to communicate. Still, I will now discuss different types of flames and their general meaning. Use this as a guide to decipher what is occurring during your candle magick.

## Normal Flame

When your candle is burning with a regular flame that is clean and even suggests the magick is working. It might take a while and not be as dramatic as you expect, but the intent you carry can still manifest in your life with a calm flame.

## Strong Flame

Having a tall and robust flame is a good sign as it depicts a great deal of energy and spirit around you and your ritual. If you are burning a candle to contact a deity, an intense flame suggests that the deity hears you and is listening. The spell is going well, and there is a good chance it will succeed in powerful, unexpected ways.

## Weak Flame

Having a weak flame is not a good sign when it comes to candle magick. It suggests there is a force against your intent. When you have a weak flame, think about your magick and the spell you are conducting. Is it too vague or long? Have you prepared the ritual correctly?

It doesn't mean that all is lost. If you focus, channeling more energy and creating more intent, you may start to see the flame grow stronger. If not, you may need to redo the magick a few more times. Remember to prepare correctly.

If you have a weak flame, this might mean that forces are opposing your magick. Perhaps ask yourself why. You should never conduct magick to harm or upset others. If you do, expect there will always be powers that challenge this magick. Bear this in mind when experiencing an unusually weak flame.

## Flame Goes Out

When your flame goes out during a spell, it suggests that powerful energy is working against you. Again, be aware of your intent of the spell. Could it be that it will harm or disturb another? The earth might be rejecting this magick to protect others.

If your spell is asking for something, the deity you are contacting has likely rejected the request. Perhaps it wasn't clear, or your candle was not charged properly. Give yourself a few days to think about why the flame might have gone out, be more careful and concise with your intent, and then start over. Ponder if and why you need to conduct this spell at all.

## Flame Relights Itself

When a flame relights itself, it means that there is still work to be done by you for your spell to be fulfilled. Something is not ready yet for the magick to occur, and you need to work this out. The magick will be possible, though, sometime in the future.

## A Jumping or Dancing Flame

This type of erratic flame suggests high energy. There is an explosion of magick, but this is not always a good sign. This energy might mean resistance if you are conducting a spell directed towards another person. It means you need to put more intent behind your magick.

If there is a long, dancing flame, this suggests the magick will be successful, but there can be complications. This is something that we are all vulnerable to when it comes to magick, but know that there will be a reason for these complications.

## A Crackling Flame

When there is crackling or chattering coming from your flame, this suggests some sort of communication with outside forces. Something or someone in the universe answers you back, and you must try and work out what is being said.

If the crackling is intense, frequent, and aggressive, it means spirits or souls could be fighting back. Perhaps you are conducting a ritual against someone who has put a hex on you. They know you are attempting to reverse this hex and trying to stop you. Concentrate on the spell and the intent with more of your energy.

If the crackling is soft, this might be a gratitude from the universe or an acknowledgment of your requests. Sometimes these noises are ancestors or spirits trying to contact you. Try and connect back, opening up yourself to communication.

# 9

## SPELLS TO GET STARTED

Of course I'm not going to leave you hanging. I've put together a nice collection that spans different types and uses. Performing the spell is the best part, isn't it?

**Personal Spells**

**Easy Candle Spell**

**Items Needed**

- 1 Candle
- 1 Metal Candle Holder
- Grapeseed Oil or Virgin Olive Oil

**Directions**

Begin by selecting a candle whose color is appropriate for your goal. Different colors symbolize different things, for instance, if you choose to use this spell to increase your money, you would go for a green candle, since green signifies money, abundance, prosperity.

Get the candle and, at equal distant, create seven grooves in it. Using your choice of oil, dress the candle, rubbing the oil on it from the middle to the bottom, then the middle to the top.

Set the candle in the candle holder and light the candle. Focus on your goal while the candle burns to the first groove. Burn the candle each evening to the following groove until it has completely burned out.

You can as well write out what you want, even in rhyme and burn it after reciting it as a chant. Save any ashes and wax and make into a ball as a Talisman or save in a spell box in the event you wish to reverse the spell.

**Basic Candle Spell**

**Items Needed**

- Candle
- Paper (same color of candle)
- Candle Holder
- Cauldron or Fire-Safe Bowl

**Directions**

One of most simple form of candle magick Select what your objective is. Write it down on the colored paper. Here is an example. For a success spell, write down your goal. Something similar to "I am worthy of success and attract it with every choice I make. I will come to be financially prosperous. I am powerful, inspired, and passionate." In some practices, you would write your objective in a magickal alphabet, such as Theban, Runic, Enochian or Malachim. Since this is a success spell, a gold piece of paper would be best, along with a gold candle. While you write down your goal, imagine yourself attaining that goal. Meditate on the various ways in which your objective might manifest. Could you be receiving a raise at work or have your own business?

After you write your goal down, fold the paper towards you, focusing on your goal the entire time. Some individuals like to say a little incantation while they do this. Does this sound like you? It doesn't have to be anything elaborate. You can use something as straightforward as:

*"Achievement is what I desire and demand*

*Hear now, this is my command*

*Success I know I will surely see*

*As I will it, so it shall be."*

Put one corner of the folded paper in the flame of the candle. Let it catch fire. Short of burning your fingers, Hold the paper as long as possible and then place it in your cauldron or fire-safe bowl to burn the remainder of the way by itself.

Let the candle to burn out entirely then dispose of it by burying it outdoors or whatever method you decide on.

### Simple Love Spell

### Items Needed

- White Tea Candle
- Pillar Plate

### Directions

Light candle and place it by the window sill at night.

This is represents you calling out to your love. I particularly love the effortlessness of this spell.

### Love Spell

**Items Needed**

- 1 Pink Candle
- 100% Virgin Olive Oil
- Candle Holder
- Stylus, Sharp Knife or Straight Pin

**Directions**

Place a pink candle on a table or your altar. As you dress the candle with olive oil, fill the candle with love and desire. Imagine love and direct all your emotion and feelings into the candle.

After dressing the candle, take a stylus pen, knife or straight pin and carve what it is you desire into the candle. Light candle and allow it to burn out.

**A Confidence Candle Spell**

**Items Needed**

- Pink Candle
- Pink and White Rose Petals
- Candle Holder
- Spring Water

**Directions**

Improving your own opinion of yourself can go a long way in giving you confidence in any part of your life. On an altar or table, make a ring of flower petals and set up the candle in the center. Before you light it, think of your best traits and concentrate on those for a few minutes. Light the candle. Repeat the following:

*"May my own light shine*

*With love and divine."*

Take a long drink of water, to cleanse out your negative thoughts of yourself. Leave the candle to burn out on its own

## Friendship Candle Spell

### Items Needed

- Pink Candle
- White Silk Ribbon
- Pink Silk Ribbon
- Good Luck or Friendship Oil
- Candle Holder

### Directions

After casting your circle, arrange your altar. Petition the goddess and God that will be joining you. You will want to dress the pink candle with Good Luck or Friendship oil as you think of the friends you want to meet. Visualize yourself going out with them, laughing with them, simply having fun. Actually picture yourself with them.

Once you have dressed your candle, light it. Call out the factors that are vital to you in a friend. While you light the candle, imagine the flame as being the energy which happens between two close friends. After this is done, take the two pieces of silk ribbon and intertwine them together.

As you are doing this, reflect on bringing that friend nearer to you. This binding method is similar to the Handfasting rituals. You will be binding that friend to you. Having them dependable and loyal to you. The way any good friend ought to be. Do not to bind an exact person to you. It's considered to be magick that's harmful because it harms the other person's free will. You only want to bind the notion of the perfect friend to you.

After you have completed this, tie the ribbon to the bottom of your candle as well as you can. The light from the candle is to be a beacon to create a friendship to you and another person. When this is finished, you might want to sit and meditate on the spell. Send out your energies to bring the perfect friend to you. When you feel that your spell has been done, then it has been. Allow your candle burn completely out and release your circle as you thank the Goddess and the God.

## Quick Candle Healing Spell

### Items Needed

- 1 Blue Candle
- Stylus, Sharp Knife or Straight Pin
- Candle Holder

### Directions

Moving from the base to the blue candle to the tip, use the stylus pen, knife or straight pin to inscribe the name of the individual who is ill. Penetrate the candle with the pin and leave it there. Allow the candle burn down completely and extinguish itself.

## Dream and Seeing Spell

### Items Needed

- 1 White Candle
- Black Marker
- Small Silver or Purple Square Fabric
- Amethyst Gemstone
- Candle Holder

### Directions

Draw an eye on the candle, the fabric and stone with the marker. Put everything on your altar and light the candle.

Place the stone on the fabric so the eyes you've drawn are touching. Imagine an eye on your own forehead with the intention of it opening to look into your dreams. Press the fabric to your forehead, with the drawing of the eye against your skin.

Stare into the candle, and speak "open my sight" again and again as you look at the candle's flame. Place the fabric back on the table, and afterward allow the candle burn down on its own. When you finished, you can sleep with the fabric below your pillow for clairvoyant dreams.

## A New Start Candle Spell

### Items Needed

- 2 White Taper Candles
- Rosemary Oil
- 2 Candle Holders

This is a good multi-purpose spell that can be used to give a bit of "enthusiasm" to any new enterprise, whether it's a new job, relationship or just a new chapter in your life.

### Directions

Anoint both candles with some oil, and set them in candle holders next to each other. Light one of them, and describe some of the "outdated" things you are hoping to get rid of. Focus on them for a few minutes, and then use the candle flame to light the second candle. Snuff out the first one.

List some of the new things that you are hoping to draw into your life at this new start. Be optimistic but realistic too. Leave the second candle burning until it is finished. You can reuse the first candle in another spell if you want.

## Spells for the Home

### Home Blessing Candle Spell

### Items Needed

- 3 Purple or Blue or Candles
- 3 Sticks Frankincense Incense
- 3 Sticks Sandalwood Incense
- 3 Sticks Rosemary Incense
- 3 Copper Pennies
- 3 Candle Holders
- 3 Incense Burners or Censers
- Bell

### Directions

The candles must to be large enough so a penny will squeeze in the candle holder beneath them. Place the candles in an equal triangle, putting one penny in each of the candle holder, beneath the candle.

Ignite the first candle and speak "Bring to me hope", at that time light the sandalwood incense. Ring your bell.

Ignite the second candle and speak "Bring to me peace", at that time light the frankincense incense. Ring your bell.

Ignite the final candle and speak "Bring to me good luck", then light the rosemary incense. Ring your bell one concluding time.

Place the incense burners or censers inside your candle triangle and allow everything burn for at about an hour. Extinguish the candles once you are finished.

## Simple Space Cleansing

**Items Needed**

- Blue Taper Candle
- Square of White Paper
- Salt
- Candle Holder

### Directions

To keep negative energy out of your space. It is a suitable spell for one room, instead of your whole house. Lay the paper out on your altar or table, and set up the candle in the center of it. Use a clear glass candle-holder if you have one, though any type will do. Sprinkle a circle of salt around the paper, so that all 4 corners of the paper are just touching the salt.

Light the candle right at the top of the hour, and let it burn right down. When it's done, carefully brush the salt onto the paper, and pour it down the drain. Bury the paper outside. All the bad energy in the room is now gone.

## Room Candle Cleanse

**Items Needed**

- White Candle
- Salt
- Candle Holder

### Directions

Put the candle in the center of the room. Scatter the salt in a ring clockwise around the candle. Ignite and say:

*"Being of wax*

*Being of fire*

*Pay attention to me*

*And listen to my desire*

*Clean this room*

*Using the power of three*

*Eject and release all negativity*

*With harm to none*

*So mote it be."*

Allow candle to burn for at about an hour.

## Spells for Protection

### To Stop Harassment

### Items Needed

- Brown Image Candle
- Piece of Paper
- Pen
- Pillar Plate
- Stylus, Sharp Knife or Straight Pin

### Directions

During the waning moon, use the brown image candle to signify the individual who is harassing you. On the front as well as back of the candle write the individual's name. On a little piece of paper, write:

Starting this point on, (name) will speak nothing but sweet words to me and about me.

*"By the power of Aradia, daughter of Diana*

*This is my will, so mote it be!"*

Place a drop of honey in the center of the paper and roll it into a ball. Heat a stylus, sharp knife or straight pin, create a slash in the candle's mouth and fill the paper ball into it.

Let the candle burn a slightly for a while for an odd number of evenings, with a maximum of nine evenings. Toss the leftovers into flowing water, but keep some candle drippings or ash to scatter in the path of your persecutor.

Candle Binding Spell

Items Needed

- Large White Candle
- Picture or Image of the Person and whatever you wish to bind them from
- Sea Salt
- Dried Rosemary
- Dried Sage
- Black Thread
- Tray
- Pillar Plate
- Optionally Items:
- Red Ink
- Purple Ink
- Pieces of Paper

Directions

Grind and mix dried rosemary and sage. Get the large white candle and place it on a tray. Stick to it a picture or any other image of the individual you are binding. Create a circle of sea salt about it. Create a second circle with your rosemary and sage mixture. Load the remainder of the tray with pictures that signify what you wish to bind the individual from. However if the issue is too difficult for pictures, write whatever the individual is bound from on pieces of paper and put them about the candle. If you are sad, purple ink and if you are angry, use red ink. Wrap the candle and the picture with the black thread.

Speak aloud whatever you are binding this individual from. Ignite the candle and allow it burn up until the wax starts to drip over the image and thread.

You will burn it each day for a week, while waiting for the picture to be heavy with wax. Work this as a meditation method to point your will to bind the individual. You will have direct results if you have a just reason for this spell. You can also bind a person from harming himself or herself.

**To Reverse Spells Cast With Candle Magick**

**Items Needed**

- 2 Black Candles
- 2 Candle Holders

**Directions**

Light the two black candles and chant:

*"In the name of the Gods and of all Spirits*

*In the name of Cernunnos and the light and the dark*

*And the Gods of the Netherworld*

*And whosoever is casting a curse against me*

*Let them suffer their own curse*

*Let my candles become their candles*

*This burning become their burning*

*This curse become their curse*

*Let the pain they have caused me and mine*

*Fall upon them."*

Do this spell for five consecutive nights, as close to midnight as possible, and each night chant the spell until the candles are used.

## Bye Bye Tension Spell

### Items Needed

- 4 Different Colored Candles
- 1 Pink Candle
- 5 Candle Holders
- Fresh Basil
- Sandalwood Incense
- Clear Quartz

### Directions

It's ideal to perform this spell in the middle of your home, but if that's not possible, you can perform this spell on a table or your altar. Position the five candles in a circle. Place the crystal in the middle with the mound the basil leaves on top.

Light the candles next light the Sandalwood incense, and move it all through the central rooms of your house. Taking your time, allow the smoke disperse out. When you've completed that, put back the incense to the area with the candles, and allow everything to continually burn until they extinguish out on their own. You will discover that the anxiety and conflict lifting soon.

Note: you cannot assume that magick is going to fix everything. If there are particular active difficulties going on in your home, you'll need to work them out beforehand.

**Burn Away the Negativities**

**Items Needed**

- 1 Black Candle
- Dried White Sage
- Dried Mint
- Dried Basil
- Sandalwood Oil
- Candle Holder

**Directions**

Take dried herbs and Chop them up so they are in tiny pieces. Wipe sandalwood oil all over your candle. Roll the candle in your herbs making sure they fix across the sides of the candle.

Place up the candle in the holder and light it. It might spark a little as the oil and herbs start to burn, so choose a location that is safe. As it burns, repeat three times:

*"I remove you negative energy,*

*I get rid of you bad attitude,*

*I dismiss you poor spirit*

*I accept peace and happiness."*

Allow the candle completely burn down. If there is any wax left over, bury it outside.

## Spells for Money and Abundance

### Obtaining a Job Candle Spell

**Items Needed**

- Large Green candle
- Large Red candle
- 2 Pillar Plates
- Stylus, Sharp Knife or Straight Pin

### Directions

Use this spell only after you have given in your application or resume. With a stylus pen, knife or straight pin, inscribe the company's or companies' name you have a desire to join on the side of the green candle. On the red candle, inscribe your full name and the victory rune Tiwaz, (↑) on the side. Burn both together candles on Thursday for approximately 30 minutes once the sun sets, as you visualize yourself obtaining the type of job you desire. At the conclusion of the 30 minutes, extinguish the candles.

Burn these candles each Thursday following that for approximately 15 minutes until you obtain the job or they burn out. Get rid of the candles and place little bowl of milk outdoors overnight as an offering.

### My Career Spell

**Items Needed**

- 1 green candle
- Candle holder
- Stylus, Sharp Knife or Straight Pin

## Directions

Engrave on a green candle the type of job you want and burn the candle as you say:

*"Ensure for me this deed*

*Bring to me the job I need*

*Allow the candle to burn out completely*

*As my will*

*So mote it be."*

## A Lucky Witch Candle Spell

### Items Needed

- Orange Candle
- Cinnamon or Clove Oil
- Candle Holder

## Directions

At midnight, anointed candle with cinnamon oil or clove oil. Ignite the candle and repeat three times:

*"With brimstone, moon, witch's fire,*

*Candle light bright spell,*

*It's Good luck shall now I acquire,*

*Work your magick well.*

*Midnight twelve is the witching hour,*

*Bring the luck that I seek.*

*By wax and wick now work your power*

*As these words, now I speak.*

*Hurting none, this spell is now done.*

*As my will, so mote it be!"*

## Cross Quarter Days Spell

### Items Needed

- 9 White Candles
- 6 Green Candles
- 1 Gold Candle
- 16 Candle Holders
- Pine Oil
- Salt

### Directions

Can be performed four times a year. This spell is to start the initial minute of the two equinoxes, and the two solstices, also known as cross quarter days. This is on the night of Oct 31 (Nov. Samhain) and Jan 31 (Feb 1- Imbolc) April 30 (May 1- Beltane), July 31 (Aug 1-Lammas), starting at12:01 a.m.

Each candle should be dressed using pine oil and positioned as follows:

The gold candle is positioned in the middle of your altar. Next, set the green candles in a ring around the gold candle. Lastly, place the white candles in a ring around the green candles.

On your selected day, at a minute past midnight, draw a salt ring around the furthest circle of candles, the white candles. Ignite the gold candle first, and then moving clockwise, light the green candles. Finally, light the white candles, still moving clockwise.

Circle the altar/table clockwise three times, reciting:

*"Circling Jupiter three times the sun, bring money to me on the run."*

Do this chant three times. Sit silently for 20 to 30 minutes, visualizing your monetary needs.

In reverse order, snuff the candles out. Do not blow out or pinch or you may scatter the energies.

**Bill Money Spell**

**Items Needed**

- 1 Green Candle
- Money Drawing Oil
- Small Piece of Paper
- Candle Holder

**Directions**

On the piece of paper, write the sum you owe on a bill. Anoint your candle with the money drawing oil. Set the paper beneath the candle.

Light the candle, breath in deep. For approximately 15 minutes, you will focus imagine that you are writing the full amount on the check to pay the bill. Putting it in an envelope with a bill and then mailing it.

Extinguish the candle using a snuffer or with your fingers. Blowing out the candle will obstruct your spell.

Repeat the ritual for a week at the same time every day. On the last day, use the flame of the candle to burn the paper. Once the paper has burned completely, let the candle finish burning out on its own.

## Abundance Candle Spell

### Items Needed

- Green Candle
- Candle Holder
- Vanilla Oil or Extract
- Cinnamon Oil
- Large Denomination Coin
- Stylus, Sharp Knife or Straight Pin

### Directions

The power of the flame will assist in drawing new financial prospects to you. Using a stylus pen, knife or straight pin, carve the word "Wealth" lengthwise sideways on the candle and then anoint "Wealth" with the vanilla oil/extract and cinnamon oil. Place the coin in the bottom of your candle holder, then set the candle on top of the coin. Ignite the candle and allow it to burn completely down.

When the candle is completed, place the now wax-covered coin in a secure location to help bring about money into your life.

## A Financial Flame

### Items Needed

- Gold Candle
- Green Candle
- Patchouli Incense
- Pine Incense
- Several Acorns (or Smooth Stones)
- Piece of Paper
- 2 Candle Holders

**Directions**

On the bottom of each candle, carve the rune **Fehu** (ᚠ). Set them up in candle holders across from each other. Set the patchouli incense up next to the gold candle, and the pine next to the green one. Light everything and get the incense smoldering.

Draw another Fehu on the piece of paper, and put your acorns (or stones) on top.

Let the candles both burn down until they are completely done, and leave the acorns or stones out on the altar until some extra money comes your way.

# CONCLUSION

I am touched and overjoyed that you have made it to the end of this book. Magick is such an important part of my life, and I only wish others to have access to the wonder behind it. I wrote this book to help beginners, no matter who you are, what beliefs you hold, or what traditions you value. Magick is for everyone, as it comes from the earth and the universe. It is the natural and cosmic power that we all have access to. All things are connected, all the elements, the planets, and the soil we walk upon. Magick is in everything—energy flowing through the universe to our souls.

Developing my magical powers helped my life immensely. It can do that for you too. Open yourself up to the powers that you can grow from this journey. Think about the change you can make for yourself and others. Magick helps personal growth, inner peace, and wisdom. It assists with decision making, helping us down our paths in life. It is universal but ultimately so personal. We can develop our own spells and rituals. We can find what we need in candle magick.

I hope this book has helped you. I hope now you are at a basic understanding of candle magick and what you can achieve with it. I hope you return to this book time and time again, using it to assist you in your future practice.

Be creative, thoughtful, passionate, and most of all, have fun! Enjoy candle magick and all you can achieve.

# BIBLIOGRAPHY

Basic Candle Spell c 2014 – Witches Of The Craft®. https://witchesofthecraft.com/2023/04/09/basic-candle-spell-2/

Confidence Candle – Luna's Grimoire. https://lunasgrimoire.com/confidence-candle/

February 21, 2012 – Witches Of The Craft®. https://witchesofthecraft.com/2012/02/21/

How To Remove Wax From Candle Stick - just-candles.net. https://just-candles.net/how-to-remove-wax-from-candle-stick/

March 22, 2014 – Witches Of The Craft®. https://witchesofthecraft.com/2014/03/22/

Money Drawing 7 Day Candle to Attract Wealth & Prosperity. https://original-botanica.com/money-drawing-multicolor-7-day-prayer-candle

Spells to Get Ex Back - Powerful Voodoo Magic Spells. https://powerful-voodoomagicspells.com/spells-to-get-ex-back/

White Magic - A Candle Binding. https://www.whitemagic.ca/spell/A-Candle-Binding.html

# ABOUT THE AUTHOR

**Monique Joiner Siedlak: Author, Witch, Warrior.**

With storytelling infused with mysticism, modern paganism, and new age spirituality, Monique awakens your potential. Initiated into the craft at 20, her 80+ books explore the magick and mysteries of life.

A Long Island native, she now calls Southeast Poland home but remains a citizen of Mother Earth.

Beyond her pen, Monique craves new experiences and cherishes nature, advocating for animal welfare.

Join her captivating journey as she transports you to enchanting realms and empowers your own transformative path. Unleash the dormant magic within and embrace the extraordinary with Monique Joiner Siedlak's evocative words.

To find out more about Monique artistically, spiritually, and personally, feel free to visit her **official website.**

www.mojosiedlak.com

facebook.com/mojosiedlak

x.com/mojosiedlak

instagram.com/mojosiedlak

youtube.com/@MoniqueJoinerSiedlak_Author

tiktok.com/@mojosiedlak

bookbub.com/authors/monique-joiner-siedlak

pinterest.com/mojosiedlak

# MORE BOOKS BY MONIQUE

**African Spirituality Beliefs and Practices**

Hoodoo

Seven African Powers: The Orishas

Cooking for the Orishas

Lucumi: The Ways of Santeria

Voodoo of Louisiana

Haitian Vodou

Orishas of Trinidad

Connecting with your Ancestors

Blood Magick

The Orishas

Vodun: West Africa's Spiritual Life

Marie Laveau: Life of a Voodoo Queen

Candomblé: Dancing for the God

Umbanda

Exploring the Rich and Diverse World

**Divination Magic for Beginners**

Divination with Runes

Divination with Diloggún

Divination with Osteomancy

Divination with the Tarot

Divination with Stones

**The Beginner's Guide to Inner Growth**

Astral Projection for Beginners

Meditation for Beginners

Reiki for Beginners

**Mastering Your Inner Potential**

Creative Visualization

Manifesting With the Law of Attraction

**Holistic Healing and Energy**

Healing Animals with Reiki

Crystal Healing

Communicating with Your Spirit Guides

**Empathic Understanding and Enlightenment**

Being an Empath Today

**Life on Fire**

Healing Your Inner Child

Change Your Life

Raising Your Vibe

**The Indie Author's Guides**

The Indie Author's Guide to Fast Drafting Your Novel

**Get a Handle on Life**

Get a Handle on Stress

Time Bound

Get a Handle on Anxiety

Get a Handle on Depression

Get a Handle on Procrastination

**The Holistic Yoga and Wellness Series**

Yoga for Beginners

Yoga for Stress

Yoga for Back Pain

Yoga for Weight Loss

Yoga for Flexibility

Yoga for Advanced Beginners

Yoga for Fitness

Yoga for Runners

Yoga for Energy

Yoga for Your Sex Life

Yoga to Beat Depression and Anxiety

Yoga for Menstruation

Yoga to Detox Your Body

Yoga to Tone Your Body

**The DIY Body Care Series**

Creating Your Own Body Butter

Creating Your Own Body Scrub

Creating Your Own Body Spray

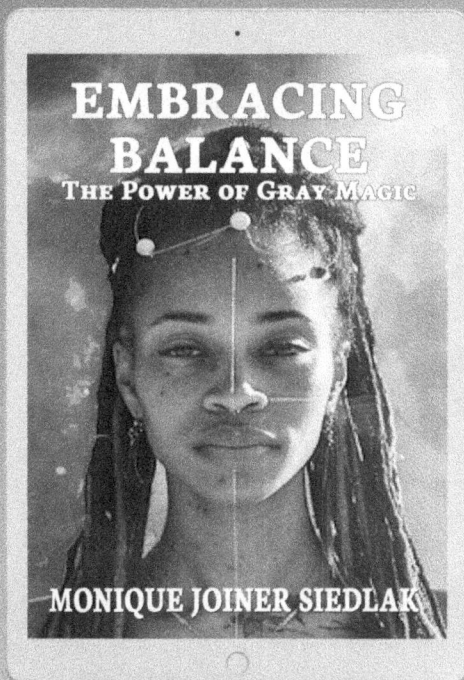

# SUPPORT ME BY LEAVING A REVIEW!

goodreads

amazon

BookBub

Download on
Apple Books

GET IT ON
Google Play

nook
by Barnes & Noble

Rakuten
kobo

www.ingramcontent.com/pod-product-compliance
Lightning Source LLC
Chambersburg PA
CBHW071622040426
42452CB00009B/1436